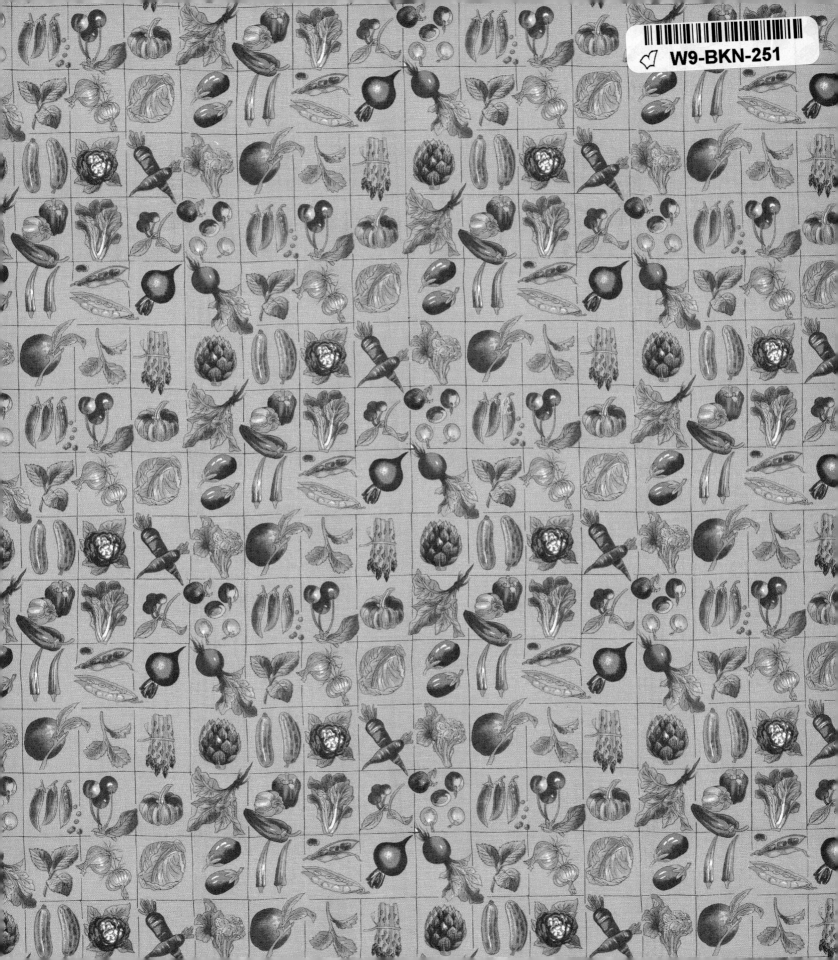

Beni's Family Cookbook

FOR THE JEWISH HOLIDAYS

This book belongs to:

_____

Jane Breskin Zalben

Beni's Family Cookbook

FOR THE JEWISH HOLIDAYS

WRITTEN AND ILLUSTRATED BY

JANE BRESKIN ZALBEN

Foreword by Joan Nathan

HENRY HOLT AND COMPANY   •   New York

I wish to thank the following cooks for their family recipes: my mother, Mae Breskin; my mother-in-law, Sara Zalben; many aunts on both sides; my pals Rahel Musleah, Johanna Hurwitz, and Barbara Shore; synagogue members Roberta Harris and Mardi Braun; and, especially, Steven Zalben—my best friend and husband—and my sons, Alexander and Jonathan—all three official tasters, helpers, master chefs, and critics. I also want to thank my grandmothers, long gone. Without the memories of the smells and tastes of their cooking, there would be no book. And there really would be no book if not for my editors, Brenda Bowen and, especially, Christy Ottaviano.

Henry Holt and Company, LLC • *Publishers since 1866*
115 West 18th Street • New York, New York 10011
Henry Holt is a registered trademark of Henry Holt and Company, LLC

Published in Canada by Fitzhenry & Whiteside Ltd.,
195 Allstate Parkway, Markham, Ontario L3R 4T8.

Library of Congress Cataloging-in-Publication Data
Zalben, Jane Breskin.
Beni's family cookbook for the Jewish holidays / Jane Breskin Zalben;
with a foreword by Joan Nathan.
p.   cm.
Summary: Present recipes arranged around twelve Jewish holy days, with
background information and anecdotes from the author's Beni stories.
1. Cookery, Jewish—Juvenile literature. 2. Holiday cookery—Juvenile literature.
[1. Cookery, Jewish. 2. Fasts and feasts—Judaism.
3. Literary cookbooks.] I. Title.
TX724.Z35 1996   641.5'676—dc20   95-51203

ISBN 0-8050-3735-7 / First Edition—1996
Printed in Hong Kong
3 5 7 9 10 8 6 4 2
Typography by Jane Breskin Zalben
The text of this book was set in Bembo.
The illustrations were done with a 000 brush in watercolors.
Country Kitchen pattern used on the book jacket and endpapers
reproduced courtesy of Hoffman California International Fabrics.
Border on pages 58 and 59 was inspired by the Barcelona Haggadah, ca. 1350.

To my family—
I wish you lives as sweet as rugelach,
and as warm and filling as chicken soup.
With all my love forever.

AUTHOR'S NOTE

My husband has been a vegetarian for more than twenty years, so we eat healthy. That means very few eggs, no salt or sugar, and hardly any oil or butter. But when the Jewish holidays come, I get nostalgic for all the traditional foods that I grew up with—the recipes I watched being made at eye level by my mother. The smells conjure memories as I cook—from entering my grandparents' apartment in Brooklyn to helping my father's mother make a batch of blintzes for the whole family when she'd come up from Miami Beach. My mother-in-law has continued the endless holiday meals, the kind in which one asks midway, "Where's the seltzer?"

As I had children, our entire family took part in the cooking. The children did what they could at their age-appropriate level—measure, sift, stir—and as they grew older the tasks became more complicated. We've enjoyed the various dishes associated with each holiday, although many recipes can overlap. For instance, tsimmes could be for Rosh Hashanah as well as Passover. Noodle kugel could be anytime, except Passover. I could eat matzoh ball soup any day of the week. What can I say? I love it. Over the years, family and friends have shared Shabbat dinners and Pesach seders over fluffy *kneidlach* or the perfect brisket, appreciating one another's secret recipes.

In all the Beni books—a series of children's books that I have written for the Jewish holidays—there is a food scene. It is out of my love for cooking, gardening, drawing, and writing—all the tiny details of living within a family and making a home together—that this book was compiled. The whole *gonsah mishpoche*—family, Beni's and mine—have pivotal roles in this cookbook. Enjoy. *Hag semeach!* Happy holidays!

FOREWORD

The illustrations in Jane Breskin Zalben's Beni books have delighted young children for years. Through the signature recipes in her various children's books, she has brought the Jewish holidays and the festival foods to young Jewish cooks everywhere. Now, in *Beni's Family Cookbook*, she has gone one step further. The author's interest in cooking has been expanded to provide a children's guide to the Jewish holidays. As she takes us through Rosh Hashanah, Chanukah, and Passover by way of her kitchen, young readers will recognize the voices of Beni and his family, as well as the often hidden voice of Ms. Zalben herself.

JOAN NATHAN, *consultant*

The ingredients for the recipes in this book include milchik (dairy), fleishik (meat), and pareve (neither meat nor dairy). As Jewish dietary laws vary according to affiliation and family origin, when in question, please consult your rabbi.

BENI'S FAMILY TREE

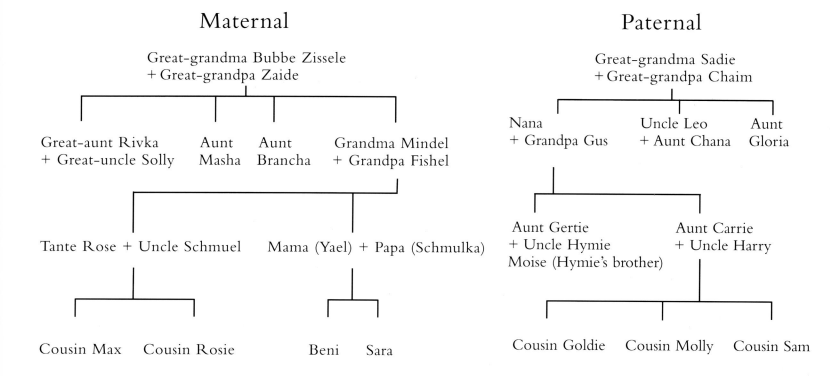

Maternal

Great-grandma Bubbe Zissele
+ Great-grandpa Zaide

Great-aunt Rivka
+ Great-uncle Solly

Aunt Masha

Aunt Brancha

Grandma Mindel
+ Grandpa Fishel

Tante Rose + Uncle Schmuel

Mama (Yael) + Papa (Schmulka)

Cousin Max

Cousin Rosie

Beni

Sara

Paternal

Great-grandma Sadie
+ Great-grandpa Chaim

Nana
+ Grandpa Gus

Uncle Leo
+ Aunt Chana

Aunt Gloria

Aunt Gertie
+ Uncle Hymie
Moise (Hymie's brother)

Aunt Carrie
+ Uncle Harry

Cousin Goldie

Cousin Molly

Cousin Sam

Roberta, Mardi, Rahel (Rabbi's wife), Manny—friends from synagogue
Rebecca, Johanna—Mama's friends
Leo and Blossom—friends and neighbors of Beni and Sara
Pearl and Avi—friends of Beni and Sara
Edie—neighbor and friend of Leo and Blossom
Clara—Bubbe Zissele's friend
Mattie—Grandma Mindel's best friend

CONTENTS

Beni's Family Cookbook

SHABBAT

Shabbat begins before sundown on Friday and ends after sundown on Saturday. It is a time to stop working and rest peacefully. "In the six days the Lord made heaven and earth, and on the seventh day He ceased His work and rested." In a way, Shabbat is a holiday every week!

The Hamotzi is a prayer said over two uncut loaves of challah (egg bread). As they are uncovered, the following blessing is recited:

Blessed are You, Lord our God,
Ruler of the universe,
who brings forth bread from the earth.

Baruch atah Adonai,
Eloheinu melech ha-olam,
hamotzi lechem min ha-aretz.

בָּרוּךְ אַתָּה יהוה
אֱלֹהֵינוּ מֶלֶךְ הָעוֹלָם,
הַמּוֹצִיא לֶחֶם מִן הָאָרֶץ.

SHABBAT

Braided Challah
Gloria's Vegetarian Chopped Liver
Grandma's Chicken Soup
Grandma's Matzoh Balls
Mindel's Gedempte Chicken
Mama's Mandelbrot

Braided Challah

After the blessing over the bread, Beni and his family rip the bread apart and dip the pieces into a tiny dish of salt. "The salt reminds us of the salt used by the priests in the Temple, and how we work and sweat to earn our food before us on the table," says Papa.

2 packages dry yeast
Pinch of sugar
3 large eggs
1 egg white (reserve yolk)
1 teaspoon salt

2 tablespoons vegetable oil
⅔ cup honey
8 cups unbleached white flour
Sesame or poppy seeds (optional,
   challah can be plain)

1. Dissolve yeast in 2 cups warm water around 105 to 115 degrees. Add sugar. Stir. Set aside 10 minutes at room temperature until liquid foams.
2. Beat eggs and egg white. Add salt, oil, and honey to mixture. Continue to beat.
3. Put flour in a large bowl. Make a well in center. Gradually add yeast mixture to flour, stirring center with a wooden spoon until absorbed. Stir in liquid from Step 2.
4. Knead dough by hand. Sprinkle lightly with flour if dough is sticky.
5. Place dough in a large bowl. Cover with a dish towel and leave near a warm spot until dough is doubled in size, about 2 hours.
6. Punch down and knead dough.
7. Divide dough into two halves. Divide each half into two pieces. One about one third of the dough, the other, two thirds. Form each large piece into three 12-inch ropes. Braid ropes. Pinch ends of ropes together.
8. Shape each smaller piece into three 10-inch ropes. Braid. Place on top of larger braids. Press braids together at the ends to seal.
9. Mix reserved egg yolk with 1 teaspoon cold water. Brush on loaves to glaze.
10. Sprinkle sesame or poppy seeds. (The seeds get stuck between Goldie's teeth just like when she makes *hamantaschen*. She loves them anyway.)
11. Let braided dough rise uncovered for 1 hour until doubled in size.
12. Preheat oven to 375 degrees. Bake for 20 to 25 minutes or until golden brown.

Yield: 2 loaves for the traditional Shabbat meal

Sunday morning, if there's leftover challah, Goldie and her family make French toast. Beat 2 eggs with 2 tablespoons milk. Add 1–2 teaspoons cinnamon and a pinch of allspice. Dip challah into batter. Soak both sides of bread. Fry in margarine. Serve with maple syrup.

Gloria's Vegetarian Chopped Liver

Beni's great-aunt Gloria serves this delicious spread with little slices of party rye bread or pumpernickel. Uncle Hymie and Aunt Gertie were in shock when they first tried it. They screamed, "It tastes like real chopped liver. Go know."

3 medium eggs
Vegetable oil for frying
3 small onions, sliced
2 ½ cups fresh green beans
¼ cup chopped walnuts
Pinch of salt and pepper

1. Boil eggs 15 minutes or until shells crack slightly. Cool and peel.
   Set aside in the refrigerator for an hour to cool.
2. Cover bottom of small frying pan with oil. Heat oil, and sauté onions until tender.
3. Steam or boil green beans until soft. Set aside to cool to room temperature.
4. Blend all ingredients in either a grinder or food processor. Mash together in a mixing
   bowl with a fork. Add salt and pepper.

Yield: 2 cups

Grandma's Chicken Soup

Grandma's chicken soup (also known as Jewish penicillin) is simple to make. Grandpa is watching his schmaltz *intake. "Please," he says to Grandma, "my arteries are hardening just looking at the soup." Skim off the fat, plop in those matzoh balls, add a little* lokshn *(noodles), and slurp.*

1 chicken (about 4 pounds)	Pinch of salt (optional)
1 large carrot, peeled	1 small onion stuck with 3 cloves
1 celery stalk with leaves	1 cup thin egg noodles (optional)
Sprig of dill	Matzoh balls (optional)

1. Put chicken in an 8-quart pot. Add 1 gallon water.
2. Add carrot, celery, dill, salt, and cloved onion.
3. Boil chicken until water is yellow and meat is tender and almost falling off the bones (about 2 hours).
4. Remove from heat. Cool. Drain vegetables and chicken from soup.
5. Refrigerate. A layer of fat will rise and harden at the top of the liquid. (This is known as *schmaltz*.) Skim off with a spoon. (Sometimes Grandma pours the soup into containers and leaves them in the freezer for an hour to hasten the process.)
6. Boil soup again. Add matzoh balls and thin egg noodles if you'd like.

Yield: 6 to 8 generous portions

Grandma's Matzoh Balls

Max's grandma told him a secret: "The key to fluffy kneidlach (matzoh balls) is the seltzer. If you add this, darling, they will never sink in your stomach like bowling balls. Remember the time Papa made them? No one could get up from the table!" But Zaide still thinks his are the best. His secret: "Keep the lid on and don't peek in the pot." Try both secrets for the perfect matzoh ball. It couldn't hurt. By the way, the grandparents are watching their cholesterol, so there's no oil, chicken fat, or soup stock in the balls.

3 large eggs
Pinch of salt and pepper

1 cup matzoh meal
¾ cup club soda or seltzer

1. Beat eggs. Add salt and pepper.
2. Pour into matzoh meal and mix by hand with a spoon.
3. Stir in club soda. Mix while it foams.
4. Cover. Refrigerate for up to an hour.
5. With your hands, form dough into balls the size of Ping-Pong balls or smaller. A trick to making smooth matzoh balls is dipping your fingers into a bowl of cold water before rolling each ball.
6. Drop balls one by one into boiling chicken soup. Boil 15 minutes, covered. Lower heat and simmer if they begin to fall apart.
7. Before serving, sprinkle soup with a tiny bit of chopped parsley or dill.

Yield: 16 matzoh balls. Serves 6 to 8.

Cousin Max would like to eat the whole pot himself! So Grandma often doubles the recipe.

Mindel's Gedempte Chicken

Mindel says, "There is something very soothing about Gedempte Chicken. It's food from my child-hood." Mindel's mama always added green peas, which she cooked right in the pot. This is delicious with little baby potatoes, or over a bed of brown rice.

2 large carrots, peeled
1 large celery stalk, sliced
1 chicken (about 4 pounds) cut in eighths
1 small onion

3 cloves garlic
2 teaspoons paprika
Pinch of pepper
Potatoes, peas, or rice (optional)

1. Slice carrots and celery into half-inch slices.
2. Put chicken, carrots, celery, onion, and garlic into an 8-quart pot. Add about two inches of cold water to pot. Sprinkle paprika and pepper over chicken parts.
3. Cover pot. Stew over low flame for 1 hour, or until the chicken and vegetables are tender. If you want to be like Mindel's mama, also add about 8 to 10 little red potatoes and about ½ cup of peas to pot. Serve over 2 cups or more of cooked rice.

Yield: Serves 6

Mama's Mandelbrot

Beni's grandparents love to dip mandelbrot *(almond bread) in a glass of tea. "When the dough gets a little hard the next day,"* Grandma says, *"I could nearly plotz it's so delicious! And the almonds, heaven."* Mandelbrot *is great for Shabbat because it stays fresh several days!*

4 large eggs
1 ½ cups sugar
1 teaspoon vanilla extract
½ teaspoon almond extract
Pinch of cinnamon
½ cup vegetable oil

¼ teaspoon salt
3 cups unbleached white flour
1 tablespoon baking powder
¼ teaspoon grated lemon rind
½ cup whole almonds
½ cup slivered almonds

1. Preheat oven to 350 degrees.
2. In a large bowl, beat together eggs, sugar, vanilla and almond extracts, and cinnamon.
3. Add oil and blend.
4. Into a separate bowl, sift salt, flour, and baking powder together.
5. Add grated lemon rind to dry ingredients above.
6. Gradually add dry mixture to wet. Blend thoroughly.
7. Chop whole almonds in a blender or food processor. Mix with slivered almonds.
8. Fold nuts into dough. Pour batter into three 4½ x 9-inch greased pans. The trick is to not pour batter more than one inch deep in pan.
9. Bake 45 minutes. Cut into ½- to 1-inch slices.

   Yield: 3 loaves (Slice immediately! How thick you slice will determine how many oblong cookies there will be.)

ROSH HASHANAH

Rosh Hashanah—which means "Head of the Year"—is the Jewish New Year that arrives in September. The holiday is the Birthday of the World and marks the beginning of the Days of Awe (also called the Days of Penitence), which end with Yom Kippur, the most solemn day of the year. Rosh Hashanah and Yom Kippur are called the High Holy Days. The *shofar,* a ram's horn, is blown many times during the service to announce the new year. *Tashlikh,* a ritual in which bread crumbs are tossed into a body of water, symbolizes the casting away of sins to start the new year afresh. *L'shanah Tovah Tikateivu* is a greeting, meaning "May you be inscribed for a good year." Apples are dipped in honey to wish that the coming year will be sweet and good, and special holiday meals are served with sweet ingredients.

ROSH HASHANAH

Tante Rose's Round Raisin Challah
Sara's Sweet Potato Tsimmes Pudding
Roberta's Brisket
Zissele's Rugelach
Mardi's Honey Cake Muffins

Tante Rose's Round Raisin Challah

Sara likes to help Tante Rose bake challah. While Tante Rose mixes the ingredients, she tells Sara that "The round challah symbolizes the cycle of life and its seasons. It is also said to be like a ladder to heaven. The bread is more special than the braided Friday-night Shabbat challah not only because of its shape, but because it is dipped in honey instead of salt, so the new year will be sweet and filled with joy." Sara loves the sweet part best.

2 packages of dry yeast	2 tablespoons vegetable oil
Pinch of sugar	⅔ cup honey
3 large eggs	9 cups flour (about)
1 egg white (reserve yolk)	½ cup raisins
1 teaspoon of salt	½ tablespoon cinnamon

1. Dissolve yeast in 2 cups warm water around 105 to 115 degrees. Add sugar. Stir. Set aside 10 minutes at room temperature until liquid foams.
2. Beat eggs and egg white. Add salt, oil, and honey to mixture. Continue to beat.
3. Put flour in a large bowl. Indent center. Gradually add yeast mixture to flour, stirring center with a wooden spoon until absorbed. Stir in liquid from Step 2.
4. Mix by hand. Fold in raisins and cinnamon. Sprinkle lightly with flour if the dough is sticky. When dough is smooth, place in a greased bowl. Cover bowl with a dish towel. Keep in a warm place for 1 to 2 hours, until doubled in size. Punch down.

5. Knead for about 5 minutes on a floured board or surface until the dough tightens and is not sticky. Divide into 3 balls. Form each ball and roll into a snakelike rope about 18 inches long. Shape circle by twisting each rope into a spiral with the end at the top of the center.

6. Let it rise again uncovered for 1 hour on a greased pan or cookie sheet until doubled in size.

7. Preheat oven to 375 degrees.

8. Brush loaves with mixture of beaten egg yolk and 1 teaspoon cold water.

9. Bake for 20 to 25 minutes or until golden brown.

Yield: 3 loaves

Sara's Sweet Potato Tsimmes Pudding

Every February, Beni and Sara help Papa tap sap from the maple trees in their backyard. They boil down the sap, then pour the syrup into little glass jars, which they give as shalach manot, *gifts of food to friends and relatives during Purim. Whatever is left, they save for Rosh Hashanah and Passover recipes like this. Mama says, "If you don't have a maple tree or your own beehive, store-bought syrup or honey is fine."*

5 medium sweet potatoes or yams
½ teaspoon ground nutmeg
½ teaspoon ground ginger
½ teaspoon cinnamon

⅓ cup maple syrup or honey
2 tablespoons grated lemon rind
2 to 3 apples, diced (peeled or unpeeled)
8 to 10 pitted prunes, chopped

¾ cup pineapple chunks
2 medium carrots, peeled and cut into ⅜-inch thick slices
miniature marshmallows (optional)

1. Bake sweet potatoes on a cookie sheet in 400-degree oven 1 hour until soft. Cool.
2. Scoop out inside of potatoes into a mixing bowl. Stir in spices.
3. Add maple syrup or honey. Sprinkle with fresh lemon rind and mix.
4. Fold in fruit and sliced carrots.
5. Grease a 7½ x 12-inch baking pan. Spoon in sweet potato mixture.
6. Bake 30 minutes at 350 degrees or until apples are soft but not runny like applesauce. Sometimes, Sara dots the top of the pudding with miniature marshmallows before baking. Beni likes the larger size. Mama says, "It's sweet enough with just the potatoes!"

Yield: Serves 10 to 12

Roberta's Brisket

One holiday, Mama and Papa were invited to their friend Roberta's home. The brisket was a real hit with everyone, but Roberta was embarrassed to reveal the secret ingredients—jelly and ketchup—until Mama dragged it out of her.

1 first-cut kosher beef brisket
  (about 4 to 6 pounds)
8 to 10 ounces ketchup
4 ounces grape or black currant jelly
1 small onion, chopped
3 large cloves garlic, chopped
2 celery stalks cut into 1-inch slices
3 carrots cut into 1-inch slices
20 baby potatoes (optional)
Pinch of paprika
Sprig of fresh parsley, chopped

1. Put brisket in a very large pot on stove top. Smear with ketchup and jelly. Add 1 cup boiling water and all vegetables.
2. Cook, covered, for at least 2 hours. Remove brisket from pot and slice in thin $\frac{3}{16}$-inch horizontal strips. Return meat to pot and continue to cook until it is tender and soft. This can be done on the stove or in a baking dish inside the oven at 350 degrees.
3. Baby potatoes are a perfect addition to the brisket. They can be boiled and peeled, or roasted, unpeeled, with a little oil and garlic and then added to the pot after meat has been sliced. Add a pinch of paprika and a sprinkle of fresh parsley, and the dish is perfect!

Yield: Enough for about 6 to 8 good eaters

Zissele's Rugelach

Dough

2 sticks (1 cup) unsalted margarine or butter
1 8-ounce package cream cheese
½ teaspoon vanilla
½ teaspoon salt (optional)
2 cups unbleached flour

Filling

⅔ cup walnuts or almonds, chopped
⅓ cup granulated sugar
½ cup raisins or currants
1 teaspoon cinnamon
Strawberry or red raspberry jam

1. Let margarine or butter and cream cheese soften at room temperature. Cream together with a hand mixer or in food processor, adding vanilla.
2. Add salt to flour. Sift flour.
3. Gradually add flour to creamed mixture while blending.
4. When sticky dough is formed, knead it for five minutes on a floured surface. Wrap dough in waxed paper, and refrigerate until it hardens, at least ½ hour.
5. Preheat oven to 350 degrees.
6. Remove from refrigerator. Divide dough into 3 parts. Then roll on a floured surface until dough is 9 to 10 inches wide by 18 inches long by ⅛ inch thick. In a small bowl, mix nuts with sugar, raisins or currants, and cinnamon.
7. Smooth a thin layer of jam over each sheet of pastry. Sprinkle ⅓ of the sugar-nut mixture on surface. Roll up dough like a jellyroll. Roll should be 1¾ inches wide. Slice into ¾-inch strips. Repeat with other rolls. Gently dust with extra sugar and cinnamon.
8. Place rugelach on a greased cookie sheet. Bake for 20 to 25 minutes. The color of the rugelach should remain light tan and the bottom of the pastry soft.

Yield: About 5 dozen

Mardi's Honey Cake Muffins

3 cups sifted flour
1 teaspoon baking soda
1 teaspoon baking powder
4 medium or 3 large eggs, separated
1 cup sugar
¼ cup vegetable oil
Juice of one lemon
1 cup honey

1 cup strong coffee
1 teaspoon ginger
1 teaspoon cinnamon
1 teaspoon allspice
1 teaspoon cream of tartar
¾ cup white raisins
1 tablespoon grated almonds
Whole or slivered almonds, raisins (garnish)

1. Preheat oven to 350 degrees.
2. Sift flour, baking soda, and baking powder together. Set aside.
3. Beat egg yolks and sugar until foamy. Add oil, lemon juice, honey, and coffee. Mix well. Combine with dry ingredients.
4. Mix in ginger, cinnamon, and allspice.
5. In another mixing bowl, beat egg whites with cream of tartar until stiff and peaks are formed.
6. Fold egg whites into batter with spatula. Gently stir in raisins and grated almonds until egg whites are no longer visible.
7. Grease or paper-line muffin tins. Pour batter ⅔ full to allow muffins to almost double in height.
8. Sprinkle 3 slivered almonds on top of each muffin, or decorate with 1 large raisin or 1 whole almond.
9. Bake for 25 minutes.

Yield: 24 muffins

YOM KIPPUR

Yom Kippur is a day of atonement. On this day we ask God to forgive us for all the wrong things we have done. We make peace with ourselves and promise to try and be better in the coming year. The holiday, lasting twenty-four hours, is devoted to repentance, prayer, reflection, and fasting. On Erev Yom Kippur, the night before the holiday, a traditional meal is served before sundown. On Yom Kippur night, after sundown, a light brunch-style feast, with dairy, vegetables, and kugels, is served to break the fast, often called a Break-Fast Meal.

YOM KIPPUR

Grandpa's Babaganoush
Fishel's Falafel
Rivka's Kasha Varnishkas
Solly's Knishes
Gus's Bagels
Walnut-and-Raisin Spread

Grandpa's Babaganoush

Grandpa says it's best to make sure the tahini is thoroughly mixed before you measure. Sometimes the oil rises to the top of the jar and the bottom paste is like thick chunky peanut butter. Grandpa turns the jar upside down an hour or two before he makes his babaganoush (eggplant salad). (Tahini can be bought at any health food store or quality supermarket.)

1 large eggplant
¼ cup tahini (sesame paste)
Juice of one lemon
Salt and freshly ground pepper to taste
¼ teaspoon ground cumin or to taste

1 teaspoon olive oil
Pinch of cayenne pepper
Italian parsley, chopped
3 to 4 pita breads

1. Wrap eggplant in aluminum foil. Put on a tray to prevent dripping.
2. Bake for 1 hour at 400 degrees. Drain in a colander as it cools. Scoop out soft insides. Whip vegetable with whisk or fork in a bowl.
3. Add tahini, lemon juice, salt and pepper, cumin, olive oil, and cayenne pepper.
4. Beat mixture until smooth.
5. Serve on platter as an appetizer. Around the babaganoush place marinated tuscan peppers, cherry tomatoes, black olives (Grandpa calls them "muslinas"), cucumber slices, stuffed grape leaves, and pickled beets.
6. Garnish the eggplant with finely chopped Italian parsley. Serve with warm pita bread sliced in wedges. Use the bread to dip and scoop babaganoush.

Yield: Serves 4 to 6

Fishel's Falafel

Mama thinks falafel (chickpea patties) is also another great meal for Chanukah, especially if you fry it in olive oil. By the third night of Chanukah, Mama has had "enough with the latkes."

1½ cups chickpea flour
½ to ¾ cup bulgur cracked wheat
2 tablespoons chopped parsley or
   chopped cilantro
Pinch of salt (optional)
¼ teaspoon black pepper
Pinch of cayenne pepper

¼ teaspoon garlic powder
¼ teaspoon onion powder
¼ teaspoon turmeric
¼ teaspoon cumin
¼ cup warm seltzer
1 cup warm water
Vegetable oil for frying

1. Mix together flour, wheat, herbs, and spices. Stir in seltzer and 1 cup warm water. Set aside 30 minutes until a paste is formed. With your hands, form balls the size of large walnuts.
2. Deep-fry balls in oil. Fry until each side is light golden brown. Cover pan to prevent splattering. For low-fat falafel, bake in preheated 400-degree oven. Turn balls until they are evenly lightly browned.
3. Stuff falafel in a warm pita pocket along with chopped salad (lettuce, diced tomatoes, and cucumbers) and tahini or hot sauce. If you'd like to make your own hot sauce, combine 2 diced tomatoes, 1 finely chopped onion, 1 diced jalapeño pepper, finely chopped cilantro (to taste), and 2 to 3 tablespoons of white vinegar. Just like a salsa— Hot! Hot! Hot!

Yield: 21 balls

Rivka's Kasha Varnishkas

Beni's great-aunt Rivka, his grandma's sister, serves this recipe of noodles and buckwheat groats the night before Yom Kippur, Erev Yom Kippur. After sundown, the family fasts. None of the grown-ups eat a single thing until the next night at sundown. Beni's grandma likes to have kasha varnishkas at the Break-Fast Meal, the night ending the holiday. She traditionally serves a dairy meal, and this makes a great dish! One Yom Kippur, Beni couldn't hold out, so after going to the synagogue, he had a little nosh. He felt sad when Grandpa caught him. "Don't worry," Grandpa said, "you haven't become a Bar Mitzvah. After you're thirteen, then worry!" So Beni figured he had a couple of years left before he had to fast like the grown-ups.

1 cup kasha (roasted buckwheat kernels)	2 tablespoons vegetable oil
1 cup bow tie noodles	1 teaspoon salt
1 small onion, minced	1 teaspoon pepper

1. In an uncovered pot, boil 2 cups water. Add kasha and cook 10 minutes, or until kernels are soft. Drain.
2. In a separate pot, boil 2 cups water. Add noodles and cook for 15 minutes. Drain.
3. In a small frying pan coated with oil, sauté onion for about 5 minutes or until onion is soft. Add salt and pepper.
4. Mix together kasha, noodles, and onions. Serve.

Yield: Serves 6 to 8

Solly's Knishes

Rivka's husband, Sol, usually uses kasha filling for his knishes. You can, too—just follow the directions for Rivka's varnishkas, leaving out the noodles. Knish dough is similar to rugelach dough, so Sol uses the rugelach recipe, but leaves out vanilla. When Rivka isn't looking, he throws in an extra pinch of salt. Over the years, by adding a little bit of this and taking out a little bit of that, Great Uncle Sol (known to the family as Solly) has come up with his own recipe. Recently, Sol discovered that the younger family members are not big kasha mavens, so he stuffs some of the knishes with mashed potatoes. One year he used farmer cheese and blueberries. Rivka threw her arms up and cried, "Is this a knish or a blintz?"

Filling

4 large baking potatoes, peeled and cubed
½ cup low-fat milk
Pinch or two of salt
⅛ teaspoon pepper

Dough

1 cup butter or margarine, softened
8 ounces cream cheese, softened
1 large egg, beaten
2 cups flour, sifted

1. Preheat oven to 375 degrees.
2. Boil potatoes until soft. Mash by hand or with a hand mixer.
3. Add milk, salt, and pepper, and mix until smooth. Set filling aside.
4. In another bowl, blend butter, cream cheese, and egg.
5. Gradually add flour. (Sometimes Solly adds a touch of water if the pastry is crumbly.) Knead dough over itself on a floured surface.
6. To prevent sticking while forming a ball of dough, sprinkle additional flour on hands.
7. Slice dough in half and roll out both halves into 8 x 16-inch rectangles. Slice in half widthwise. Fill center with kasha or potato, leaving about a 1-inch border. Roll up both like a jellyroll. Slice into 4-inch knishes and pinch sides to hold filling.
8. Place smooth side up in a greased baking pan. Bake 10 minutes, then turn over and bake 10 minutes more, until lightly browned on both sides.

Yield: This recipe varies according to the size of the knish. Sol likes big knishes. He got eight out of this recipe. If you like mini-knishes, the quantity is naturally much larger. "Experiment! That's what cooking is all about!" Solly suggested.

Pareve: Substitute pareve margarine for cream cheese. Leave out the milk!

Gus's Bagels

At first, Gus thought making his own bagels seemed a bisl meshuga—a little nuts—since you can buy them anywhere. But everyone went a little crazy when they saw how easy they were to make and how delicious they were to eat!

1 package of dry yeast
1½ tablespoons sugar
1 tablespoon vegetable oil
4 cups unbleached flour
½ teaspoon cream of tartar
1 teaspoon salt
Optional Toppings:
Poppy, sesame, or caraway seeds
chopped garlic
Kosher salt

1. Dissolve yeast and sugar in 1 cup warm water. Let foam. Add oil.
2. Mix together 2 cups of the flour, cream of tartar, and salt. Blend well with yeast mixture.
3. Gradually add the rest of the flour and mix well. Form dough into a large ball.
4. Cover dough in bowl with a dish towel. Let rise in a warm spot for 1 hour. Punch down dough and knead. Allow to sit for 5 minutes.
5. Preheat oven to 425 degrees. Tear dough into 16 pieces. Roll into ½-inch thick ropes, 4 to 6 inches long for mini-bagels. For standard bagels, tear dough into 8 pieces and roll them 1 inch thick and 6 to 8 inches long. After dough is rolled, pinch ends together to form circles.
6. Boil water in a large pot. Drop a few bagels in at a time. Do not crowd. Boil one side for 30 to 60 seconds, roll over, boil other side.
7. Continue to cook for another minute. Drain bagels on a flat strainer. Leave plain or coat with seeds, garlic, salt, or whatever you like.
8. Put boiled bagels on an ungreased cookie sheet. Bake for 10 minutes, or until very pale tan.

Yield: 8 large bagels or 16 mini-bagels

Walnut-and-Raisin Spread

Gus says, "Give me a plain bagel with a plain shmeer of cream cheese, and I'll be happy. Just call me 'No-Fuss Gus.'" But Beni and Sara make a walnut-and-raisin spread, and they are even happier. "Between you and me," Gus says, "your spread tastes like a dessert, but I know your generation loves it. My generation liked it with chopped chives." "Chives!" Beni cries, as he watches Sara poke a few extra raisins onto her bagel. She is in heaven.

8 ounces cream cheese, softened
2 tablespoons sugar or honey
⅓ cup chopped walnuts
⅓ cup dark raisins
2 dashes cinnamon
1 drop vanilla extract

1. Allow cream cheese to stand for 15 minutes at room temperature. Blend all ingredients with hand mixer.
2. Place in serving dish and refrigerate.

   Yield: Serves as a spread for 6 to 8 bagels, which depends on how generous the bagels are smeared with the spread

SUKKOT

Sukkot is the Festival of Booths, or Tabernacles. It is a joyous festival that commemorates the final gathering of the harvest. A *sukkah* (a temporary booth) is built for Sukkot. In it a family eats, drinks, and sleeps during the holiday, and is reminded of how the Israelites lived in the wilderness. The booth may have three sides or four, with walls of bamboo poles or canvas, and a loose roof of tree branches of evergreens or palms. The covering of branches should be heavy enough for there to be shade during the day, but open enough for the stars to be seen at night.

There are four festival symbols, called the Four Species: palm, willow, myrtle, and etrog or citron. The waving of the *lulav* (or palm branch) in different directions symbolizes that God is everywhere.

In 1620, when the Pilgrims came to America, they held a harvest festival. They based their first Thanksgiving on the ancient holiday of Sukkot.

SUKKOT

Aunt Carrie's Stuffed Cabbage
Edie's Cranberry-Apple Bread
Nana's Pumpkin Popovers
Zaide's Pumpkin-Banana Bread

etrog (citrus fruit)

lulav (palm branch)

Fruits and Vegetables You Can Hang in the Sukkah

figs

popcorn

cranberries

peppers

gourds

tomatoes

pumpkins

cabbages

oranges

apples

lemons

peaches

pears

corn

beets

carrots

Aunt Carrie's Stuffed Cabbage

Filling	Sauce
1 medium onion, grated	16 ounces tomato sauce
2 eggs, beaten	½ cup tomato juice
2 pounds chopped meat	16 ounces jellied cranberry sauce
Pinch of salt (optional)	Juice of one lemon
½ teaspoon chili powder	¼ to ½ cup white raisins
⅓ cup uncooked rice	4 whole cloves

1 large cabbage

1. In a large bowl, combine onion and beaten eggs. Add meat, salt, chili powder, and uncooked rice. Set aside.
2. Boil water in a large pot. Core cabbage head and remove large leaves. Boil or steam 3 to 4 minutes, covered. Either way works to soften leaves.
3. Remove cabbage from pot. Drain. In the center of each leaf add 2 to 3 tablespoons of meat filling. Roll meat in leaves by folding the curved sides toward the center, one over the other. Fold up the ends like an envelope. Put on a plate. (Any extra filling can be rolled into meatballs.)
4. Combine sauce ingredients in a large bowl or casserole. Coat the bottom of dish with half the sauce. Place stuffed cabbages, seam side down, in a row. Spoon the remaining sauce over all to prevent burning.
5. Simmer on top of stove in a covered casserole or bake in 350-degree preheated oven for 1½ to 2 hours. Spoon liquid over cabbages every half hour.
6. Skim off fat. Freeze any stuffed cabbages for a later treat.

Yield: One dozen

Edie's Cranberry-Apple Bread

Whatever cranberries Edie has left, she shares with her next-door neighbors Leo and Blossom, who string them with a needle and thread, making a rope to hang across their sukkah.

1 cup fresh cranberries
¾ cup chopped walnuts (optional)
1 teaspoon grated lemon rind
1 large McIntosh apple, peeled and diced
1 extra large egg, beaten
½ teaspoon vanilla extract

2 tablespoons margarine, melted
¾ cup orange juice
1 cup granulated sugar
2 cups unbleached flour
1 teaspoon baking powder
½ teaspoon baking soda

1. Preheat oven to 350 degrees.
2. Mix cranberries, walnuts, lemon rind, and apple in a small bowl and set aside.
3. Beat egg with mixer until frothy. Continue to mix, adding vanilla, margarine, orange juice, and sugar.
4. Sift flour, baking powder, and baking soda.
5. Gradually add dry ingredients to wet, and blend until smooth. Stir in cranberry-nut-apple mixture.
6. Pour batter into a 4½ x 13-inch greased bread pan. Bake for 1 hour, or until top of bread splits slightly.

Yield: One long loaf or two smaller loaves

Nana's Pumpkin Popovers

Pumpkins are in season during Sukkot. "Canned pumpkin is okay, but there's nothing like the real thing," says Nana. She uses it for different recipes—pumpkin bread, pumpkin soup, pumpkin pie.

1 medium pumpkin or
    ½ cup canned pumpkin
½ cup vegetable oil
Pinch of salt (optional)
1 cup matzoh meal
4 large eggs, beaten
1 tablespoon honey
⅛ teaspoon cinnamon
Pinch of ground ginger
Pinch of ground nutmeg

1. Cut open pumpkin and discard pulp and seeds.
2. Scoop out flesh of pumpkin. Boil chunks in large covered pot with 2 inches water at bottom. When pumpkin is soft and stringy, it is done. Drain, cool, and mash.
3. Preheat oven to 350 degrees.
4. In a medium saucepan, stir oil, 1 cup water, and salt over low flame. Turn off heat when liquid bubbles.
5. Add matzoh meal to oil. Mix quickly until a paste forms. Cool 5 minutes.
6. In a small bowl, beat together eggs, honey, and spices. Add to matzoh paste.
7. Mix in pumpkin. With your hands, form balls the size of large plums. Dip hands in cold water in between rolling balls of dough. This makes popovers smoother and easier to mold (like the matzoh balls!).
8. Plop onto a greased cookie sheet. Bake 45 minutes. Serve warm!

Yield: One dozen

Zaide's Pumpkin-Banana Bread

When Leo and Blossom were in their sukkah *on a cool night eating dinner outside, the pumpkin bread warmed their insides and filled the* sukkah *with wonderful smells. "It reminds me of the Havdalah service at the end of Shabbat," Blossom said. She ran inside the house to get the spice box filled with cloves.*

2 cups unbleached flour
2 teaspoons baking powder
1½ teaspoons baking soda
¼ cup butter
⅓ cup dark brown sugar
2 large eggs, beaten
1 teaspoon molasses
1 cup fresh pumpkin, cooked or canned
2 large ripe bananas

½ cup sour cream
½ cup plain yogurt
¼ cup light raisins
¼ teaspoon cinnamon
Pinch of ground cloves
Dash of ginger
Dash of nutmeg
Pinch of salt
Whole almonds

1. Preheat oven to 350 degrees.
2. Sift flour, baking powder, and baking soda into a bowl. Set aside.
3. In a large bowl, cream butter and sugar. Add eggs and mix well.
4. In a food processor or mixer, blend remaining ingredients except almonds with butter-sugar-egg mixture. Gradually add flour mixture.
5. Pour batter into 2 greased bread loaf pans (about 5 x 9 inches) or 1 long large pan. Fill three-fourths full.
6. Dot top of the bread with whole almonds. Bake for at least 1 hour. Turn off heat and leave in oven to cool until center is dry and firm. Make sure top of loaf doesn't get too dark.

Yield: One or two loaves, depending upon the pan choice

SIMCHAT TORAH

On Simchat Torah the first and last portions of the Torah are read to show that the cycle of learning never stops. A *simcha* is a joyous occasion. Simchat Torah is a celebration of completion and, like Purim, it is a time to have a lot of fun. The holiday occurs after Sukkot. Everyone happily rejoices in the synagogue, parading and waving small Israeli flags, dancing, singing, and eating jelly apples.

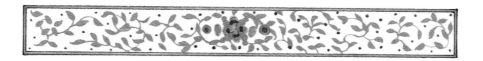

SIMCHAT TORAH

Moishe's Caramel–Nut Apples
and
Chocolate-Coconut Apples
Uncle Hymie's Jelly Apples

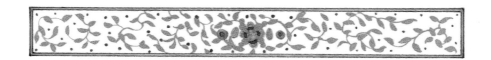

Moishe's Caramel-Nut Apples and Chocolate-Coconut Apples

"Work very quickly!" Moishe shouted as everyone dipped and turned. "They're coming out bumpy! Not like the perfectly smooth store-bought caramel apples," Blossom sighed. "Let's dip them in coconut to hide the bumps!" Leo smiled. "We don't have to." Moishe lined up the apples on wax paper. "We made them ourselves. That's the best kind of all."

1 large McIntosh apple
wooden stick

Caramel-Nut Topping	Chocolate-Coconut Topping
½ cup peanuts, chopped	¼ cup of shredded coconut
⅔ cup caramel candy, melted	⅔ cup bittersweet chocolate

Caramel-Nut Apples

1. Wash, dry, and remove stem from apple. Pierce center of apple with stick like a Popsicle.
2. In a small bowl set aside chopped peanuts.
3. In a small saucepan melt caramel candy over low heat (about 3 minutes). Turn off burner.
4. Dip apple into melted caramel, turning the apple so that its surface is generously coated. Remove apple from saucepan.
5. Dip apple into small bowl of peanuts. Turn until apple is lightly sprinkled.

Yield: One apple. Increase ingredients by the number of apples you want to make.

Chocolate-Coconut Apples

1. Wash, dry, and remove stem from apple. Pierce center of apple with stick like a Popsicle.
2. In a small bowl set aside shredded coconut.
3. Using a double boiler or saucepan, melt bittersweet chocolate over low flame (about 3 minutes). Turn off heat.
4. Dip apple into melted chocolate, turning the apple to coat surface. Remove apple from boiler or saucepan.
5. Dip apple into small bowl of coconut. Turn until apple is lightly sprinkled.

Yield: One apple. Increase ingredients by the number of apples you want to make.

If you have braces, hold off on this recipe unless you want to take a trip to the orthodontist. Otherwise, enjoy!

Uncle Hymie's Jelly Apples

"Candy making has to be done quickly because the jellied corn syrup hardens. Work carefully with a partner," says Uncle Hymie. Hymie works with Moishe.

1 large McIntosh apple
Wooden stick
Margarine or butter to coat pot
⅓ cup light corn syrup or 1 cup sugar, dissoved in ¾ cup boiling water
A pinch of cream of tartar (to bind ingredients)
1 teaspoon red food coloring

1. Wash, dry, and remove stem from apple. Pierce center of apple with stick like a Popsicle.
2. Grease pot with margarine or butter so liquid doesn't boil over. Pour in corn syrup or sugar-and-water mixture. Heat over low flame. Add cream of tartar.
3. While simmering (at least 3 minutes), boil 4 cups of water in a larger pot.
4. Dip wooden spoon in syrup. Blow on it. If syrup begins to harden, place smaller pot of corn syrup in a larger pot of boiling water (like a double boiler). Quickly add red food coloring and stir. Turn off burner and cool 5 minutes.
5. Glaze apple by twirling fruit in corn syrup mixture. (If making several apples, glaze one at a time.)

Yield: One apple. Increase ingredients by the number of apples you want to make. The more liquid in the pot, the easier it is to dip and cover apples with candy coating.

CHANUKAH

Chanukah is the Festival of Lights, which lasts for eight days. A candle on the menorah (or *Chanukiah*) is lit for each night to commemorate the Maccabee warriors' victory over the Greek forces of Antiochus. Chanukah means "dedication." There was enough oil for the Eternal Light in the Temple only for one day, but a great miracle happened: the lamp burned for eight days. The Maccabees rededicated the Temple in Jerusalem.

Potato pancakes *(latkes)* as well as many other treats are cooked in oil and eaten during this holiday.

These are the blessings as you light the candles on the menorah:

Blessed are You, Lord our God,
Ruler of the universe,
who has sanctified us by Your commandments,
and has ordered us to light the lights of Chanukah.

Baruch atah Adonai
Eloheinu melech ha-olam
asher kideshanu bemitzvotav
vetzivanu Lehadlik ner shel Chanukah.

בָּרוּךְ אַתָּה יהוה
אֱלֹהֵינוּ מֶלֶךְ הָעוֹלָם,
אֲשֶׁר קִדְּשָׁנוּ בְּמִצְוֹתָיו
וְצִוָּנוּ לְהַדְלִיק נֵר שֶׁל חֲנֻכָּה.

Blessed are You, Lord our God,
Ruler of the universe,
who accomplished miracles for our ancestors
in ancient days, in our time.

Baruch atah Adonai
Eloheinu melech ha-olam
sheh-asah nissim la-avoteinu
ba-yamim ha-heim baz'man hazeh.

בָּרוּךְ אַתָּה יהוה
אֱלֹהֵינוּ מֶלֶךְ הָעוֹלָם,
שֶׁעָשָׂה נִסִּים לַאֲבוֹתֵינוּ
בַּיָּמִים הָהֵם בַּזְּמַן הַזֶּה.

CHANUKAH

Mama's and Papa's Latkes
Applesauce
Rahel's Falouris (Indian Latkes)
Apple Chutney
Chana's Doughnut Holes
Chanukah Dreidel Cookies

Mama's and Papa's Latkes

Mama likes plain old potato latkes. Papa adds a pinch of cayenne pepper to his—Cajun-style, with a "zing" to them! Beni, on the other hand, is a "latke maven." He eats them out of season and can never have enough. He loves his Mama's latkes. Papa's too!

2 large eggs, beaten
4 to 5 large potatoes, peeled and grated
1 medium onion, peeled and grated

¼ cup matzoh meal
Salt and pepper to taste
Vegetable oil for frying

1. In a large bowl, combine eggs, potatoes, and onion.
2. Blend in matzoh meal, salt, and pepper.
3. Heat 1-inch layer of vegetable oil in a large frying pan. Drop in 1 heaping tablespoon of mixture for each latke. Turn over when crisp and golden.
4. Drain on paper towels.
5. Serve with sour cream or applesauce.

   Yield: Serves 6, depending on appetites!

Applesauce

Beni says there are two ways to eat latkes: the smear method and the dollop method. The smearer covers the entire surface of the potato pancake with sauce. The dolloper scoops a small quantity of sauce on the side and dips. Beni is a dolloper. He likes chunky applesauce and scoops it with a soup spoon!

8 large McIntosh apples, cored
½ cup maple syrup
2 cinnamon sticks

¼ cup light or dark raisins
1 lemon, quartered
Dark brown sugar to taste

1. Place whole apples in a large pot. Pour maple syrup over apples.
2. Add cinnamon sticks, raisins, and lemon wedges to pot. Sprinkle brown sugar on top of apples, according to how sweet you like them. (Beni likes them sweet.) Partially cover pot and simmer until the apples are soft and runny.
3. Either scoop out sauce from the skins and put in a bowl, or mash through a strainer, discarding apple skins. (Papa likes to eat the skins. He tells Beni and Sara, "All the vitamins are in the skins!")

Yield: Serves 6 to 8, depending on the type of latke eater.

Rahel's Falouris (*Indian Latkes*)

When Beni made these latkes with his mama and papa, they drained them on paper towels over a brown paper bag to absorb the extra oil. Beni ate one or two when no one was looking, so maybe there were really twenty latkes! Beni's friend, Rahel, serves her famous latkes with apple chutney on the side.

2 cups chickpea flour
1 teaspoon salt
1 teaspoon ground cumin
½ teaspoon cayenne pepper

1½ teaspoons turmeric
⅓ cup cilantro
1 medium onion, chopped
vegetable oil to coat frying pan

1. Mix all dry ingredients together in a food processor or bowl.
2. Add 1½ cups water and blend in food processor with cilantro.
3. By hand, or with one quick turn of the food processor, add onion.
4. Use a large serving spoon to drop mixture into an inch of hot oil in a frying pan. Fry on both sides over a medium flame about 1 to 2 minutes, or until golden brown.
5. Serve immediately (or reheat for a later treat).

Yield: 18 latkes, about 3½ inches in diameter

Apple Chutney

7 medium cooking apples (or peaches, pears, or mangoes), cored and peeled

1 tablespoon peeled and chopped ginger root

1 medium clove garlic, minced

1 teaspoon ground cloves

⅛ teaspoon cayenne pepper

1 teaspoon cinnamon

1 cup honey

½ cup orange juice

1 cup cider vinegar

1. Coarsely chop apples, peaches, pears, or mangoes.
2. Combine all ingredients in saucepan.
3. Bring to boil, then lower heat to simmer.
4. Simmer uncovered, stirring occasionally, for 1 hour.
5. Cool before storing in sealed jar. Serve on the side with latkes.

Yield: 3 cups

Chana's Doughnut Holes

Beni's neighbor Frankie bit into one and cried, "It tastes like the zeppeles my aunt Sophia makes in Italy!" In France and New Orleans, it might be called a beignet, and in Germany, a kuchen.

1 package dry yeast
¼ cup warm water
1 egg, beaten
1¾ cups milk
1 stick (½ cup) butter
¾ cup sugar

3 dashes salt
Dash of nutmeg
Dash of cinnamon
Rind of 1 lemon
5½ cups flour
Large pot of oil for frying

1. Dissolve yeast in ¼ cup warm water in a bowl for 10 minutes.
2. Add to beaten egg. Mix and set aside.
3. Scald milk in a pot. Add butter to hot milk and melt. Remove from heat.
4. When mixture is lukewarm, add sugar, salt, nutmeg, cinnamon, and lemon rind. Add beaten egg and yeast mixture.
5. Blend in flour. Knead until an elastic ball of dough forms. Cover with a dish towel. Set aside in a warm spot. Allow dough to double in size. After a few hours, punch down and rip off pieces of dough. Roll into small balls about the size of walnuts.
6. Heat enough oil for dough to float and expand in pot. When oil is bubbling, pop a few balls in at a time. Cook quickly (about 3 minutes), rolling ball around with a ladle until lightly brown all over. Drain.
7. Dust with confectioner's sugar. (Chana's trick is to put sugar in a paper lunch bag, add doughnuts a few at a time, and shake!) You can also dip them in grape jelly.

Yield: 3 dozen

Chanukah Dreidel Cookies

1 large egg yolk (reserve egg white)
1 teaspoon vanilla extract
2 tablespoons orange juice
3 cups unbleached flour
1 cup sugar
2 sticks (1 cup) unsalted butter softened to room temperature

1. In a small bowl, beat egg yolk, vanilla, and orange juice.
2. In a large bowl, combine flour, sugar, and butter.
3. Mix together and knead until dough forms ball.
4. Wrap dough in waxed paper and refrigerate for at least 1 hour. (Beni took a nap and made the cookies when he woke up!)
5. Preheat oven to 350 degrees.
6. Roll dough on waxed paper with a rolling pin until it is as thin as possible. Press in cookie cutter shapes. (Max had a dreidel. Beni had a star. Mama had a menorah. For the candles on the menorah cookies, Mama and Sara used sprinkles—a different color for each night! Crystal-colored sugar is fun, too.)
7. Glaze top of each cookie with reserved egg white, using a pastry brush or a clean paintbrush.
8. Bake 10 minutes. Watch carefully! Make sure cookies are pale white with a slightly golden edge.

Yield: 6 dozen (varies according to what shapes you make)

TU B'SHVAT

Tu B'Shvat, the New Year of Trees, is the fifteenth day of the Hebrew month, Shvat. The holiday usually falls in late January or early February, when trees form fruit. Tu B'Shvat is one of four New Years on the Jewish lunar calendar.

Seven fruits associated with the land of Israel are eaten at a special seder on this day. They are olives, dates, figs, grapes, pomegranates, wheat, and barley. Four cups of wine are sipped, just like at the Passover seder. Some Sephardic communities prepare as many as thirty or more fruits! Carob, also called St. John's Bread, is eaten on Tu B'Shvat. Its swordlike shape reminds us of the destruction of the Temple.

THE SEVEN FRUITS AND THEIR SIGNIFICANCE

olive   Olive oil was used in the Temple. The tree is a sign of hope.

date   The date palm is strong and beautiful. Its fruit is sweet.

fig   Figs ripen at different times. The whole fruit is edible. The Torah, part of the Jewish bible, has been linked to the fig tree, a symbol of peace.

grape   Grape wine is sweet and used in many ritual blessings.

pomegranate   A pomegranate's skin reminds us of the physical world hiding and protecting the jewel-like seeds of the spiritual world inside us.

wheat, barley Wheat and barley are "fruits" of the soil. These grains make bread, which is the Staff of Life.

TU B'SHVAT

Avi's Date-Nut Bread
Carob Chip Cookies
Masha's Mushroom Barley Soup
Papa's Fruit Salad

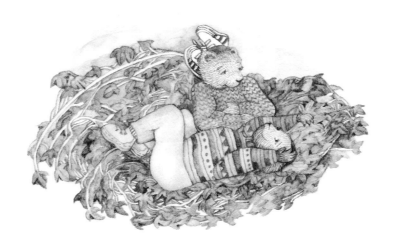

Avi's Date-Nut Bread

2 cups unbleached flour
½ cup dark brown sugar
2 teaspoons baking powder
¼ teaspoon salt
Pinch of cinnamon
Pinch of nutmeg
½ teaspoon grated orange rind

2 large eggs
½ cup yogurt
½ cup sour cream
2 tablespoons margarine
1 tablespoon molasses
½ cup chopped walnuts
¾ cup chopped dates

1. Preheat oven to 350 degrees.
2. Sift flour, sugar, baking powder, and salt into a bowl. Add cinnamon, nutmeg, orange rind, walnuts, and dates. Mix well.
3. In another bowl, combine eggs, yogurt, sour cream, margarine, and molasses. Mix well.
4. Add all wet ingredients to dry. Stir until thoroughly blended.
5. Pour dough into a 5 x 9-inch greased bread pan.
6. Bake 1 hour until bread is dry in the center. Test with a toothpick. If it comes out moist, continue to bake. If toothpick is dry, it's done.
7. Let bread stand at room temperature for 5 minutes. Bang pan gently on wooden cutting board or other hard surface to remove bread from pan. Use a knife around the edges to loosen the bread from the pan.

Yield: One loaf

Carob Chip Cookies

Beni invited his friends Pearl and Avi over to make cookies. They kept eating the chips as they went along. It's a good thing Mama put a cup aside before they began baking!

1 cup margarine, softened
⅔ cup granulated sugar
⅔ cup dark brown sugar
2 extra large eggs, beaten
2½ cups flour, sifted
1 teaspoon baking soda

Pinch of salt (optional)
Pinch of cinnamon (optional)
1 teaspoon vanilla extract
1 tablespoon water, boiling
1 cup sweetened carob chips
1 cup chopped walnuts

1. Preheat oven to 350 degrees.
2. In a mixing bowl, cream margarine and both sugars. Add the eggs and mix.
3. In another bowl, sift flour and baking soda. Add salt and cinnamon. Blend.
4. Add vanilla, 1 tablespoon boiling water, carob chips, and walnuts. Stir thoroughly.
5. Drop dough from teaspoon onto greased cookie sheets. Space ¾ inch apart to allow cookies to expand.
6. Bake 10 to 12 minutes. Allow cookies to harden for a minute or so on sheet before removing with a spatula.

Yield: 5 dozen

Masha's Mushroom Barley Soup

This is a nice thick winter soup. Beni's papa is a vegetarian, but Grandpa likes to toss in a juicy piece of flanken on the bone. Of course, then the soup isn't meatless. It's up to you. Either way, Grandpa says, "I could almost eat this soup with a fork!"

½ cup dried lima beans or 1 cup frozen or fresh lima beans
2 large carrots, peeled and cut in ¾-inch slices
2 small celery stalks with leaves, chopped
7 to 10 medium mushrooms, sliced
1 large potato, peeled and diced
1 cup fresh dill, chopped
2 cups of pearled barley
Pinch of salt (optional)
Large pinch of pepper
1 ounce soy sauce or 1 vegetable bouillon cube

1. Soak dried lima beans overnight. They will swell to 1 cup by morning. You can also use frozen beans. Put lima beans into a pot filled with 4 quarts of water.
2. Put all vegetables and barley in pot of water with lima beans.
3. Add salt, pepper, and soy sauce, or vegetable bouillon cube.
4. Simmer, covered, for at least 2 hours, or until the grains are soft.

Yield: Serves 12

Papa's Fruit Salad

Beni's papa loves to make fruit salad for every holiday, but especially for Tu B'Shvat! "I guess I'm not the only baleboosteh! I'm kvelling!" Grandma says proudly. "I'm glad he's a good homemaker, too!" Mama adds. Beni and Sara eat bits of fruit as they help Papa dice and peel.

2 large apples
1 large pear
2 oranges, peeled
1 large grapefruit, peeled
2 kiwis, peeled
1 cup of fresh pineapple
2 peaches
2 plums
1 nectarine
1 to 2 fresh figs

2 bananas
6 strawberries
½ cup seedless grapes
½ cup raisins, dark or light
½ cup raspberries
½ cup blueberries
1 cup watermelon balls
½ cup cantaloupe balls
½ cup honeydew balls
coconut flakes (optional)

mint leaves (optional)

1. Chop apples, pear, oranges, grapefruit, kiwis, pineapple, peaches, plums, nectarine, and figs into bite-sized pieces.
2. Finely slice bananas and strawberries.
3. In a large bowl, combine all chopped and sliced fruit. Add grapes, raisins, raspberries, blueberries, and melon balls. Toss gently.
4. Spoon fruit salad into individual sherbet glasses or fruit-cup bowls. Sprinkle each portion with coconut flakes. Add a mint leaf on top of each serving.

Yield: Serves 12 to 15

PURIM

The story of Purim is told in the scroll of the Book of Esther at the Megillah reading. King Ahasuerus was ruler of the vast Persian Empire. He was married to Queen Vashti, but he later banished her from the kingdom for disobeying his commands. Esther, a beautiful young Jewish woman, was chosen to be his new queen. Esther's cousin, Mordecai, warned the king of a plot by Haman, his prime minister and chief adviser, to kill the king and all the Jews of Persia. Haman cast lots (*purim*) to determine the day the Jewish people would be destroyed. But Haman was stopped when Queen Esther told the king of his evil plan. Through her bravery, the Jewish people were saved, and Mordecai became a trusted adviser to the king after Haman's death.

Purim is a joyous time. It reminds us of triumph over evil and of the future of Jewry. The Fast of Esther comes the day before Purim to commemorate the day of prayer before the Jews' victory. And then, as on many holidays, a festive meal celebrates the spirit of the holiday. It is customary to give out *shalach manot* (gifts of food) to family and friends, just as Mordecai instructed all Jews to do on the first Purim.

PURIM

Goldie's Hamantaschen
Chaim's Chickpeas
Bubbe's Stewed Prunes
Aunt Brancha's Baklava

Goldie's Hamantaschen

Goldie and her mama bake batches of hamantaschen *(named after the wicked Haman) and make little packages of fruit and nuts for treats. "Why are the pastries shaped like triangles?" asks Goldie. "Some think Haman wore a three-cornered hat. Others say he had pointy ears that looked like triangles," answers Mama. (These pastries are also known as "Haman's pockets" because the Yiddish* tashn *means "pockets.")*

3 cups unbleached flour
½ teaspoon baking soda
2 teaspoons baking powder
¼ teaspoon salt
⅔ cup sugar
⅛ teaspoon cinnamon

¼ cup cream cheese, softened
½ cup margarine, softened
½ teaspoon vanilla
2 tablespoons milk
2 tablespoons orange juice
1 medium egg

½ cup filling of your choice: poppyseeds and prune or apple butter, apricot preserves, pitted cherries, chocolate chips, or minced walnuts and honey

1. Preheat oven to 350 degrees.
2. Sift flour, baking soda, and baking powder. Mix in salt, sugar, and cinnamon. Set aside.
3. Cream margarine and cream cheese.
4. Add vanilla, milk, orange juice, and egg to creamed mixture.
5. Blend well in food processor or mixer. Gradually add dry mixture and mix until a soft dough is formed.
6. Place dough on a lightly floured board or table. Flatten with rolling pin until dough is about ⅛ inch thick.
7. Cut into 3-inch circles using an upside-down glass.
8. Fill each circle with ½ teaspoon of filling.
9. Press the edge of the circle up and pinch to make triangles. Place hamantaschen on a greased cookie sheet.
10. Bake 10 minutes or until light tan.

Yield: 4 dozen

Note: This is a dairy recipe. If pareve, substitute water for milk and add ¼ cup more pareve margarine for cream cheese.

Chaim's Chickpeas

Papa likes plain chickpeas sprinkled with pepper. He pops them in his mouth as if he were eating popcorn. Mama thinks it's more festive to add the red peppers. And especially Jerusalem artichokes!

1 pound dried chickpeas, or
    16-ounce can of chickpeas
1 sweet red pepper, diced
2 teaspoons olive oil

¼ teaspoon pepper
¼ teaspoon cumin
1 (6-ounce jar) Jerusalem artichokes
Handful of Italian parsley (optional)

1. Soak dried chickpeas overnight in at least 6 cups water. Boil, covered, in same water until tender. It takes approximately 3 hours! Or you can substitute canned chickpeas.
2. Coat chickpeas and pepper with oil. Add spices. Stir in artichokes. Garnish with freshly chopped Italian parsley.

Yield: Serves 6 to 8

Bubbe's Stewed Prunes

Bubbe served the prunes for breakfast with a tiny bit of cream. Goldie likes her prunes with plain yogurt. Molly tried some on vanilla ice cream as a dessert. And Sam left his for Grandpa the following morning. To each his own!

2 cups pitted large prunes
½ cup maple syrup
2 cinnamon sticks
¼ cup light raisins
1 lemon, quartered

1. Put prunes, maple syrup, cinnamon, and raisins in a pot on top of stove.
2. Squeeze juice from lemon quarters into pot, then add the squeezed lemon rinds. Cover pot.
3. Cook on low flame 10 minutes until prunes are plump and soft.
4. Cool to room temperature. Eat plain or however you wish.

Yield: 4 servings

Aunt Brancha's Baklava

Aunt Brancha uses paper-thin strips of phyllo dough for baklava, strudel, or feta-cheese pies. She buys her phyllo at any good supermarket or specialty food store.

Pastry and Filling

1 pound almonds and pistachios
  (or substitute with walnuts)
1 to 1½ cups granulated sugar
2 teaspoons ground cinnamon
½ pound of unsalted butter or margarine
1 lb. box phyllo dough (12" x 17" sheets)

Syrup

½ cup brown sugar
½ cup honey
⅓ cup lemon juice
½ teaspoon cardamom
Pinch of ground cloves

1. Preheat oven to 350 degrees.
2. Grind nuts in blender or food processor. Stir in sugar and cinnamon.
3. Melt butter or margarine in a saucepan over low heat, being careful not to brown. Grease a 12 x 17-inch baking dish. Put 4 phyllo dough sheets folded in half on bottom of pan. (Makes 8 layers.) Brush melted butter in between each layer.
4. Spread nut mixture evenly across the top sheet of dough. Layer with another 6 sheets, brushing with butter after each layer. Continue with another layer of nuts. Repeat with remaining phyllo and nut mixture until top of pan is reached. Drip rest of butter on top and smear.
5. Score or cut squares, diamonds, or triangles to make one-inch squares. Bake 45 minutes at 350 degrees.
6. While the baklava bakes in the oven, make syrup. Pour all ingredients into a small pot with 1 cup water. Boil, uncovered, 15 minutes on medium flame until syrup is thick. Cool. Spoon over baked pastry. Let baklava stand for 30 minutes to soak up syrup.

Yield: Pieces vary according to shape and size of pastries. Makes approximately 32 one-inch squares.

PASSOVER

Passover is the Festival of Spring and Freedom. The Haggadah (which means "narration") tells the story of redemption from slavery to freedom. Rosie and Max's grandparents refer to the holiday as Pesach. There are seders the first two nights to reenact the Jewish Exodus from Egypt. During the seder meal, Rosie has many favorite rituals: asking the Four Questions; dipping her pinky in the wine while reciting the Ten Plagues; singing "Dayenu"; searching for the *afikomen* (hidden dessert matzoh); pouring a goblet of wine for the prophet Elijah; leaving the door open for him to enter; and later seeing if he has drunk from the wine cup. Most of all, Rosie loves the food, and hiding under the table as she crawls around the relatives' legs. It is a very special time of year. She and Max help set up the seder plate and learn about what each food symbolizes.

PASSOVER

Cousin Rosie's Matzoh
Yael's Apple-and-Walnut Ḥaroset
Manny's Date-and-Almond Ḥaroset
Papa's Fresh Beet Horseradish
Aunt Gertie's Gefilte Fish
Pearl's Potatonik
Sam's Vegetable Kugel
Blossom's Orange Sponge Cake
Leo's Raspberry Sauce
Schmulka's Macaroons
Molly's Meringues
Beni's Brownies
Cousin Max's Matzoh Brei

egg

shank bone

horseradish

matzoh

bitter herbs

parsley

ḥaroset

The Seder Plate

1. Egg (*beitzah*): A roasted egg symbolizes the festival offering in the Temple and the mourning of the destruction of the Temple. But the egg can also be thought of as a symbol of fertility and renewal.

2. Shank bone (*zeroa*): A scorched portion of the leg bone of a lamb represents the paschal offering, in memory of the ancient Temple sacrifice.

3. Bitter herb (*maror*): Sometimes romaine lettuce, sometimes horseradish, this recalls the bitterness of slavery in Egypt.

4. Grated horseradish (*ḥazeret*): This additional bitter herb is eaten with the ḥaroset in a matzoh sandwich (*korekh*), to show life has two sides—the bitter and the sweet.

5. *Ḥaroset:* This sweet paste of chopped apples, nuts, and cinnamon mixed with a little wine represents the mortar used by the Israelites while they labored in bondage to the Pharaohs. Haroset tempers the bitterness of the *maror*. A strip of cinnamon bark may be placed near the ḥaroset to represent the strawless clay bricks that the Israelites were forced to make in Egypt.

6. Parsley (*karpas*): A sprig of parsley represents spring, life, and hope. Dipped in salt water, the *karpas* suggests the bitterness of salty tears.

7. Matzoh: Three matzoth placed in the center of the seder plate stand for the unity of the three groups (tribes): Cohen, Levi, and Israel. (The matzoth may be put on a separate plate.) The matzoh itself is unleavened bread. It stands for the bread that was baking and didn't have time to rise when the Jews made their Exodus from Egypt.

Cousin Rosie's Matzoh

Passover, also referred to as the Feast of Unleavened Bread, lasts eight days. It begins with the search for hametz *(leavened food) and then getting rid of it from the house—a spring cleaning! Rosie and Max, along with Grandma and Grandpa, search for bread crumbs using a wooden spoon, candle, and feather the night before the seder.*

Rosie and Max make their own matzoth. Grandpa says, "For matzoh to be kosher, the whole process of making it from beginning to end must occur within eighteen minutes! The gluten in the flour cannot rise. Shemura matzoh (guarded matzoh) is made from flour that has been watched from the moment the wheat is cut until it is finally baked, making sure no contact has been made with water, preventing any fermentation. The dough shouldn't rise!" Rosie and Max felt like the Jews fleeing Egypt with their unleavened bread as they rushed to make their round handmade matzoh. Grandma kept saying, "Hurry up, darlings!" When the timer buzzed at eighteen minutes, everyone sighed, out of breath, "Done."

2 pounds unbleached white flour
1½ cups spring water

1. Preheat oven to 475 degrees.
2. Combine flour and spring water in a bowl. Knead dough. Tear off into 8 equal balls.
3. Flatten into about 7- to 9-inch circles. Smooth with rolling pin.
4. Prick with a fork, making rows of tiny holes.
5. Put on cookie sheet. Bake for 10 minutes, or until lightly tan.

Yield: 8 matzoth

Note: Unbleached all-purpose flour is not kosher for Passover.

Yael's Apple-and-Walnut Haroset

Grandma mashes the walnuts by hand the old-fashioned way: with her brass mortar and pestle, pounding them until they're ground into crumbs. Beni likes his haroset to have the consistency of a paste. Sara prefers to see the chopped walnuts and apples—chunky style. One year, Grandma threw in nutmeg and it tasted great. Papa's the one who added the maple syrup!

3 cups walnuts, minced
5 cups sweet apples, chopped
Rind of 1 lemon, finely grated

⅛ teaspoon nutmeg
1¼ teaspoons cinnamon
½ cup Concord grape wine

2 tablespoons maple syrup (optional)

1. Mix all ingredients well, either by hand with a mortar and pestle or in food processor.

   Yield: Enough for 20 guests, depending on how much is spread on a 2 x 3-inch piece of broken matzoh! The cousins always go for seconds. (The apples and walnuts come from Ashkenazic Jews, from Eastern Europe.)

Manny's Date-and-Almond Ḥaroset

3 cups dates, pitted and chopped
Rind of 1 lemon, finely grated
½ teaspoon orange peel, finely grated
1 pomegranate, seeded and diced

1 cup almonds, minced
1 cup raisins or currants
1 teaspoon cinnamon
½ cup sweet or dry red wine

1. In a large bowl, combine all ingredients. Ḥaroset can be chilled or served at room temperature.

Yield: How much each recipe serves is hard to say. Some heap ḥaroset on their matzoh, others take a little taste. There always seems to be enough for about 20 with generous portions on their matzoh sandwiches. (The dates and almonds are Sephardic, from Middle Eastern countries.)

Papa's Fresh Beet Horseradish

Rosie's papa pulled a nice large horseradish by its leaves from the garden. He had planted the top in the vegetable patch the year before. After a cold winter, the top grew and turned into a long horse-radish. This is how he made the horseradish for the bitter herbs at the seder.

3 to 4 medium beets
2½ cups white vinegar (enough for soaking beets and horseradish paste)
1 large horseradish

1. The night before boil beets until soft. Peel and grate. Marinate in 2 cups of the white vinegar. Refrigerate. (Canned beets can be used, but as Papa says, "Let's face it, it just isn't the same.")
2. Peel the horseradish and finely grate in a food processor. Open the windows! Cousin Rosie's and Cousin Max's eyes teared for a whole ten minutes.
3. Put in bowl. Add enough white vinegar (about ½ cup) to make a horseradish paste.
4. Add ½ cup drained beets per 1 cup horseradish paste. Mix together.

Yield: Every year there's enough to go around for about 20 guests. Some years less, others more. Papa finds no one is too eager to overdo it on the bitter herbs, but the sweet beets are more popular. If you want to be authentic, leave out the beets! Serve on the side of gefilte fish or on the matzoh *maror* sandwich.

Aunt Gertie's Gefilte Fish

Aunt Gertie's father used to keep a carp in the bathtub, but now Aunt Gertie goes to the fish store and buys it boned. Some years, she makes fish broth by boiling filleted fish bones, onions, pepper, celery tops, and carrots. She saves the stock, chilling it in the refrigerator. Beni's cousins laugh as jellied broth wobbles on the dish. Max says, "Yuck!" This year, Aunt Gertie says, "Let's keep it simple." So she uses boiling water instead of the fish broth to cook the gefilte fish. Uncle Hymie wants to add salt, but Aunt Gertie says, "Please, darling, I'm watching my sodium." Papa, on the other hand, likes everything spicy—Cajun style—from latkes to gefilte fish. He adds cayenne pepper and even puts a dab of hot pepper sauce on the side. Either way, the gefilte fish came out just fine.

3 pounds whitefish, skinned and boned
3 small onions, finely minced
¼ cup matzoh meal
1 large egg
1 teaspoon salt (optional)
½ teaspoon pepper
Pinch of cayenne pepper (optional)
1 beet, thinly sliced
1 lemon, thinly sliced
½ tablespoon dill, chopped (optional)
½ tablespoon parsley sprigs (optional)

1. Remove head and tail.
2. Chop fish in food processor. Gradually add onions until mixture is a fluffy paste. Set aside.
3. Stir in matzoh meal by hand.
4. In another bowl, beat egg with ¾ cup water. Add salt and pepper.
5. Mix all ingredients together.
6. Moisten hands and scoop mixture with a tablespoon, forming 2-inch-diameter egg-shaped balls.
7. Carefully drop each ball into a pot of boiling water (or fish broth).
8. Cover pot. Simmer 50 minutes.
9. Ladle each ball out. Drain off excess water. Put on platter.
10. Garnish perimeter of plate by alternating sliced beet rounds and thinly sliced lemon circles. Sprinkle chopped dill or sprigs of parsley on top of the fish balls. Refrigerate. Serve with horseradish.

Yield: 18 fish balls

Pearl's Potatonik

Potatonik is a little heavier than a kugel, according to Mama.

4 very large Idaho potatoes
3 extra large eggs
2 to 3 tablespoons vegetable oil
½ teaspoon pepper

½ teaspoon salt (optional)
⅓ cup matzoh meal
½ medium onion, minced
2 cloves garlic, mashed

1. Preheat oven to 375 degrees.
2. Peel potatoes. Shred in a food processor or by hand.
3. In a separate bowl, beat eggs, adding oil.
4. Measure in pepper and salt. Stir in matzoh meal.
5. Add onion and garlic to matzoh mixture.
6. Stir in potatoes. Pour entire pudding into a greased 8 x 12-inch baking dish. Bake for 1 hour or until golden brown.

Yield: Serves 12

Sam's Vegetable Kugel

Olive oil
1 celery stalk, chopped
1 large carrot, grated
1 small zucchini, shredded
1½ cups mushrooms, chopped
½ cup steamed beet greens
   or steamed spinach, chopped
2 large garlic cloves

Fresh sprig of dill, chopped
Handful of parsley, chopped
Pinch of pepper
Pinch of thyme
½ cup matzoh meal
2 large eggs, beaten
½ cup seltzer

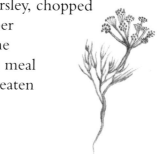

1. Preheat oven to 350 degrees.
2. In a small frying pan, heat enough oil to cover bottom of pan. Add vegetables and garlic, and sauté. Add dill, parsley, pepper, and thyme. Fry 5 to 10 minutes, or until the vegetables are slightly tender. Mash garlic when it softens. Remove from heat. Set aside.
3. Put matzoh meal in a separate bowl. Pour in frothy beaten eggs. Add seltzer and ¼ cup warm water. Stir while it foams.
4. Combine both mixtures. Spoon into greased 9-inch-square baking pan. Decorate surface with sliced mushrooms in 6 criss-crossing rows. Like tic-tac-toe.
5. Cover with aluminum foil to prevent kugel from drying out. Bake for about 1 hour. Remove foil the last 10 minutes to brown top. Cool for 10 minutes. Cut into nine 3-inch squares.

Yield: Serves 9

Blossom's Orange Sponge Cake

Blossom's grandpa shouted, "Ten eggs! Are you meshuga?" Grandma said, "I'm not crazy. Once a year, it won't kill you to eat a little sponge cake."

⅓ cup Passover cake meal
½ cup potato starch
Pinch of salt
10 eggs, separated

1 cup granulated sugar
Juice of 1 lemon
Drop of vanilla extract
Rind of 1 orange, grated

1. Preheat oven to 350 degrees.
2. Into a bowl, sift together 3 times: cake meal, potato starch, and salt.
3. Beat egg yolks until thick. Add ½ cup of the sugar, lemon juice, vanilla, and orange rind. Continue beating until foamy. Fold in dry ingredients.
4. In a separate bowl, beat egg whites. Gradually add the remaining ½ cup sugar and continue beating until stiff peaks form.
5. Using a spatula, fold egg yolk mixture into egg white mixture.
6. Pour into a lightly greased 9-inch springform tube pan. Bake 45 to 50 minutes or until a toothpick comes out clean. Turn pan upside down and cool. Serve the sponge cake with a fresh raspberry sauce.

Yield: One 9-inch cake

Leo's Raspberry Sauce

Blossom and her brother, Leo, pick raspberries from their backyard bushes each summer. Their parents freeze the berries and use them for recipes all winter long. By the spring, just enough are left for this delicious sauce.

1 cup fresh or frozen raspberries
¼ teaspoon orange rind, grated

¾ teaspoon potato starch
⅓ cup warm water

1 tablespoon of sugar or honey (or more, to taste)

1. Place berries in a small saucepan.
2. Sprinkle orange rind over berries.
3. Stir potato starch in ⅓ cup warm water and stir until it dissolves. (Substitute arrowroot or cornstarch for potato starch when it is not Pesach.)
4. Add sugar or honey to taste. Cover pot partially and steam berries about 5 to 10 minutes. Remove lid.
5. Continue to boil off excess liquid as sauce simmers and thickens. Stir about 7 minutes. Set aside to cool at room temperature or chill.

Yield: ¾ cup

Note: Once, Leo mixed the raspberry sauce with red wine vinegar and some olive oil. Oh, and a small handful of chopped basil from the garden. Yum. He got the best salad dressing in the world! Blossom called him "A culinary genius!" as she rolled her eyes.

Schmulka's Macaroons

You can add chocolate chips, maple syrup, a bit of instant coffee or cocoa, melted chocolate, or pecans for different flavored macaroons. Schmulka's is Beni's family's favorite. Simple, good, and chewy.

¾ cup whole almonds, finely chopped
1⅔ cups coconut, shredded
Pinch of salt (optional)

½ teaspoon vanilla extract
3 egg whites, beaten stiff
½ cup granulated sugar

1. Preheat oven to 325 degrees.
2. In a bowl, combine almonds with coconut and salt.
3. Add vanilla extract to beaten egg whites. Gradually add sugar to make a frothy snow. Fold into almond mixture.
4. Line an ungreased cookie sheet with aluminum foil, or use nonstick sheet. Spoon heaping teaspoons onto sheet to form cone-shaped balls. Place at least 1 inch apart.
5. Bake 20 to 30 minutes until lightly browned. Cool at room temperature and peel macaroons from foil.

Yield: 16 to 20 large macaroons

Molly's Meringues

Molly placed her meringues on brown tissue paper in a wooden-slatted strawberry basket that she got from the market. Her sister Goldie and her brother Sam thought they were mushroom caps. "They look so real!" Goldie shouted when she tasted one and realized it was dessert.

4 large egg whites at room temperature
¼ teaspoon potato starch (use cream
   of tartar when it's not Passover—
   it binds meringue together better)
¼ cup granulated sugar

1 teaspoon vanilla extract
3 ounces chocolate chips
⅓ cup chopped walnuts
⅓ cup chopped dates
Cocoa for dusting

1. Preheat oven to 225° degrees.
2. Beat ½ cup of egg whites with a mixer until frothy. Add potato starch. Increase mixer speed. When eggs begin to look like fluffy clouds, gradually add sugar. Pour in vanilla extract.
3. Turn mixer to highest speed for about 10 minutes. While mixing, line 2 cookie sheets with aluminum foil so you can peel meringues from the cookie sheet easily. Lightly grease foil.
4. Meringue is done when it sticks to a spatula in a stiff peak. Fold in chocolate chips. Add walnuts and dates, or any combination of the three. (Molly likes more chips than dates. Goldie likes the dates!)
5. Scoop a heaping teaspoon of mixture and drop onto cookie sheet. Dust top of each meringue drop lightly with cocoa. Bake slowly for 1 hour. Store in a cool, dry area.

Yield: 4 dozen

Beni's Brownies

1 stick (½ cup) unsalted butter or margarine   1 teaspoon vanilla extract
½ cup granulated sugar   Pinch of cinnamon
7 ounces semi-sweet chocolate   ¼ cup Passover cake meal
4 large eggs, separated   ½ teaspoon salt (optional)
Crushed walnuts to taste (Beni added about ⅓ cup)

1. Preheat oven to 400 degrees.
2. In a saucepan, melt butter with ¼ cup of the sugar over low heat. Stir to dissolve sugar.
3. Melt chocolate with butter and sugar. Stir until melted. Remove from heat. Set aside to cool at room temperature.
4. In a small bowl, beat egg yolks 4 minutes until thick and pale yellow in color. Add vanilla, cinnamon, and cake meal. Whisk into the warm chocolate mixture.
5. Beat egg whites with an electric mixer, slowly adding salt and ¼ cup of remaining sugar until stiff peaks form.
6. Fold egg whites into batter. Mix thoroughly by hand.
7. Pour into a greased 7 ½ x 11-inch baking dish. Dot top with walnuts. Bake 30 minutes or until top is crusty. Cool. Cut into squares.

Yield: 15 flourless brownies

Note: Passover cake meal is different from regular matzoh meal.

Cousin Max's Matzoh Brei

Rosie adds a pinch of cinnamon to her batch of matzoh brei. Her brother Max says, "Off limits with mine!" She loves to put pot cheese on the side of her matzoh brei. Rosie told the family at breakfast the morning after the first seder, "It tastes like a blintze."

3 egg matzoh
2 large eggs, beaten
Salt and pepper to taste (optional)

1. Break matzoh into small pieces in large mixing bowl. Add 1 cup boiling water. Cover bowl immediately with a dish towel to hold in steam. Keep covered several minutes until matzoh is soft. If it remains hard, add a little more boiling water. Drain off any excess liquid. Mash matzoh.
2. In a separate bowl, beat eggs until frothy. Pour over matzoh. Add salt and pepper to taste. Stir until mushy.
3. Chill in refrigerator for about 30 minutes to solidify.
4. With your hands, form dough into pancakes approximately 4 inches in diameter. Place into hot, generously greased frying pan. Once pancake is solid, turn over, fry other side until golden brown, then remove.
5. Serve with maple syrup or raspberry jam.

Yield: Serves both cousins 2 to 3 pancakes each without needing seconds, depending on thickness. For a bigger family, double the batch!

LAG B'OMER

Lag B'Omer is the thirty-third (*lag* means "thirty-three") day of the Counting of the Omer, the period between the holidays of Passover and Shavuot. Passover marks the Exodus of the Jews from Egypt and the birth of the Jewish nation. On Shavuot, the Jewish people received the Torah. Both mark physical and spiritual freedom. To recognize this link, each one of the forty-nine days between these two festivals is counted. The counting is called *Sefirat Ha'Omer.* Lag B'Omer takes place in May and is always celebrated with a large picnic. Games are often played. Bonfires are lit in Israel. A barbecue with hot dogs (Beni likes tofu pups from the health-food store!) and hamburgers or a picnic in a park are good ways to celebrate this holiday.

LAG B'OMER

Tabouleh Wheat Salad
Clara's Cucumber Salad
Shmuel's Potato Salad
Uncle Harry's Famous Coleslaw

Tabouleh Wheat Salad

1 cup cold water
⅔ cup bulgur wheat
⅛ teaspoon garlic powder
⅛ teaspoon onion powder

1 medium tomato, finely diced
Handful of Italian parsley, chopped
Juice of one large fresh lemon
1 to 2 tablespoons olive oil

1. Pour 1 cup cold water over bulgur wheat in a bowl. Add spices. Allow to stand at room temperature for 30 minutes.
2. Stir in diced tomatoes, parsley, lemon, and olive oil.
3. Serve at room temperature or chill. Great for a picnic outdoors!

Yield: Serves about 6

Clara's Cucumber Salad

1 cup white vinegar
3 large cucumbers, peeled and sliced thin
1 cup water

2 tablespoons sugar
2 tablespoons fresh dill, minced
Pinch of salt (optional)

1. Pour white vinegar in a bowl with cucumbers. In a separate bowl, dissolve sugar in 1 cup room-temperature water. Add to cucumbers and vinegar. Stir.
2. Sprinkle dill over cucumbers. Add a pinch of salt. Stir again. Cover bowl.
3. Allow cucumbers to pickle overnight in the refrigerator. Drain liquid the next day. Serve cold with a sprinkle of fresh dill.

Yield: Side dish serves 8 to 10

Note: Instead of the recipe above, Clara sometimes slices up the same number of cucumbers and adds the following ingredients: 8 ounces plain yogurt, ¼ cup chopped mint leaves, ¼ cup currants. Stir. Marinate in the refrigerator for a few hours or overnight.

Shmuel's Potato Salad

5 large potatoes

1 large green pepper, finely chopped

3 tablespoons Italian parsley, chopped

½ cup mayonnaise

2 tablespoons white vinegar

Salt and pepper to taste

1. In a saucepan, cover potatoes with water, and boil until tender. Spear gently with fork. When skin flakes off, they're done. Peel and cut into medium chunks.
2. Add chopped pepper and Italian parsley to potatoes.
3. Stir in mayonnaise and vinegar. Sprinkle with salt and pepper. Mix.
4. Cover and refrigerate for a few hours. Or serve warm if you prefer.

Yield: Serves 10 to 12 as a good picnic side dish

Note: Beni's other side of the family makes German potato salad: Leave out the mayonnaise and the parsley. Thinly slice potatoes. Add vinegar and pepper only. Uncle Hymie says, "Everyone's got an opinion. My family always adds a teeny bit of sugar. Shmuel's adds salt. Who's to argue?"

Uncle Harry's Famous Coleslaw

1 small head cabbage, grated

3 medium carrots, shredded

½ cup mayonnaise

1 heaping tablespoon sugar

½ cup white vinegar, at room temperature

1. Put cabbage and carrots into a large mixing bowl. Stir in mayonnaise.
2. Dissolve sugar into vinegar. Stir liquid. Pour into cabbage mixture. Mix thoroughly.
3. Refrigerate. Serve cold.

Yield: Uncle Harry figures it can satisfy about 10 hungry eaters along with a bunch of other side dishes or appetizers.

SHAVUOT

He brought us to this place and gave us this land, a land of milk and honey. Wherefore I now bring the First Fruits of the soil which You, O Lord, have given me.

DEUTERONOMY 26:9-10

Shavuot, also called the Feast of Weeks or the Festival of First Fruits, celebrates the giving of the Torah and the Jewish people's physical and spiritual freedom from slavery. The holy day was a pilgrimage to the Temple in Jerusalem and a harvest feast for farmers to make offerings of their first fruits: wheat, barley, grapes, figs, pomegranates, olive oil, and honey. The festival arrives exactly fifty days after Passover and lasts for two days. On the second day, a story about harvest, The Book of Ruth, one of five biblical scrolls, is read. Shavuot is one of three major agricultural festivals. The other two are Sukkot and Passover. Shavuot takes place in June when the earth is in bloom. Dairy products are eaten to symbolize how the Torah nourishes the mind as milk nourishes the body. On this holy day, synagogues and homes are often decorated with flowers, greens, and fruits.

SHAVUOT

Sadie's Blintzes

Rebecca's Samosas

Mattie's Noodle Kugel

Uncle Leo's Lox, Eggs, and Onions

Johanna's Cheesecake

Sadie's Blintzes

On Shavuot it is customary to have a dairy meal. Blintzes are often served with sour cream. Beni likes his plain, and loves to sneak a taste of the filling while he stuffs the blintzes. Sadie makes a whole batch when she comes up from Florida each summer, and freezes some for the family to last them through the winter for Sunday morning breakfasts. That's a lot of blintzes!

Batter	Filling
4 large eggs	1 pound cottage cheese
1 cup milk	7½ ounces farmer cheese
1 tablespoon sour cream	¼ cup sugar
1 tablespoon sugar	¼ cup raisins (optional)
½ teaspoon vanilla extract	½ teaspoon cinnamon
2 cups of flour	Margarine for frying

1. Beat eggs, milk, and ⅓ cup water in a bowl. Add sour cream, sugar, and vanilla. Blend.
2. Gradually add flour and mix until the batter is smooth. Set aside.
3. In another bowl, mix all ingredients for the filling. Set aside.
4. Heat a crepe or omelette pan, or a 9-inch frying pan with curved sides. Grease pan with margarine. Ladle 2 to 3 tablespoons batter into center of pan. Quickly tilt the pan in all directions until the entire bottom is covered with batter, forming a nice large pancake.
5. Cook for about a minute until the batter looks almost rubbery but not golden brown. Flip over and cool on a dish towel. Use a metal spatula to help nudge blintze along if it sticks. Add more batter and repeat process. Use margarine as necessary while frying to prevent blintzes from sticking to the pan.
6. Fill center of each pancake with 2 tablespoons of cheese mixture. Roll sides up, one on top of the other like an envelope, forming triangles at the tips. Fold triangles toward center to make a rectangle of 2½ x 4 inches. Flip blintz over onto a large plate. Do this one by one until batter and filling are used up.
7. Fry blintz in margarine until golden brown on both sides.

Yield: About 15

Rebecca's Samosas

Samosas can be fried for Chanukah, or baked for Shavuot, because of the cheese filling. Rebecca also makes these for Purim, filling them with cheese and spinach. The bitter taste of the spinach reminds us of the evil Haman.

Dough	Filling
½ cup vegetable oil	2 large eggs, beaten
¼ teaspoon salt	½ pound mozzarella cheese, grated
4 to 5 cups flour	½ pound Syrian or feta cheese
Pinch of baking powder	(Syrian cheese tastes better)

1. Bring ¼ cup warm water, oil, and salt to boil. Remove from heat. Quickly stir in flour and baking powder until consistency is that of pie dough.
2. Knead dough until smooth, adding more flour if needed.
3. Shape into about 48 balls the size of walnuts. Place in bowl and cover with a dish towel for 1 hour.
4. Roll each pastry ball flat to ⅛-inch thickness with rolling pin. Take an upside-down glass, approximately 3 inches in diameter, and stamp circles in pastry pieces.
5. Preheat oven to 400 degrees.
6. Mix eggs with cheeses.
7. Fill pastry circles with 1 teaspoon of filling. Fold into turnover shapes (crescent half circles). Seal edge with cold water, pinching carefully so cheese filling doesn't leak out when baking.
8. Bake on a greased cookie sheet 15 minutes.

Yield: 4 dozen

Mattie's Noodle Kugel

½ pound extra wide egg noodles
½ pound cottage cheese
3 ounces farmer cheese
1 cup sour cream
2 large eggs, beaten
½ teaspoon cinnamon
1 tablespoon sugar

Juice of ½ lemon
3 large apples, peeled and cored
1 dozen dried apricots, quartered
⅓ cup white raisins
3 tablespoons margarine or butter
¼ cup cornflake crumbs (optional)
¼ cup toasted ground almonds (optional)

1. Preheat oven to 350 degrees.
2. In a large pot, bring water to a boil. Add noodles. Boil until noodles are soft. Drain. Set aside in large mixing bowl.
3. In another bowl, mix cheeses and sour cream together. Pour eggs into cheese mixture. Stir.
4. Sprinkle in cinnamon and sugar. Add lemon. Stir again.
5. Cut apples into medium-size chunks. Mix all fruit together.
6. Combine fruit with noodles and cheese. Scoop into a greased 9 x 12-inch baking dish. Dot top of noodle pudding with dabs of margarine or butter blended with cornflake crumbs and toasted almond mixture (optional). Cover pudding with aluminum foil. Bake for 45 minutes. Raise oven temperature to 375 degrees and bake an additional 15 minutes, uncovered, to make it crispy.
7. Allow to cool on rack about 30 minutes. Cut into squares.

Yield: Serves 8 to 10 healthy portions

Uncle Leo's Lox, Eggs, and Onions

Mindel's mama used to wrap a nice warm faynkukhn, *which means omelette in Yiddish, for her to take to school when she arrived in America from "the old country." On Sunday mornings, her uncle Leo would say to her, "I'll make you a Leo." Anyone who knows anything knows that when you're frying an omelette of lox, eggs, and onions, you're making a L-E-O. This is how it goes.*

Slice of lox, diced
½ small onion, chopped
Margarine
Pinch of pepper
2 large eggs, beaten

1. Sauté lox and onion with margarine in a pan over low flame until onions are soft and translucent and lox is thoroughly cooked. Sprinkle with pepper.
2. Pour beaten eggs over mixture. Do not stir. Allow to simmer. When the bottom is firm, flip over and cook the other side for a minute until eggs appear solid.

Yield: One serving

Leo likes his omelette with a "glass tea" (a metal cup holding a boiling glass of tea), but it's not complete without a piece of rugelach! One day, Goldie came over and loved the breakfast so much, Leo called her "Goldie Lox" ever since.

Johanna's Cheesecake

"Sometimes the top of the cake splits, so I cover the surface with sliced strawberries," Johanna tells Sara. "I like to sprinkle some powdered sugar on top, and a few shreds of bittersweet chocolate," says Sara. "And one tiny mint leaf," adds Johanna. "From my greenhouse window." "This is getting fancy-schmancy," Sara says and smiles.

Crust

1 egg yolk, beaten (reserve egg white)
½ teaspoon vanilla extract
½ cup butter (room temperature)
Pinch of nutmeg (optional)
¼ cup sugar
1 cup flour

Filling

1 pound cream cheese, softened
1 cup sugar
2 tablespoons flour
¼ teaspoon salt
1 teaspoon vanilla extract
4 eggs, separated
1 cup heavy cream

1. Preheat oven to 400 degrees.
2. In a large bowl, mix egg, vanilla, butter, and nutmeg.
3. Gradually add sugar and flour until dough is formed. Roll into ball. Refrigerate for 1 hour. Divide dough in two and flatten one half against bottom of a 9-inch spring-form pan.
4. Bake for 10 minutes to lightly tan crust. Remove and cool for 10 minutes.
5. Flatten remaining dough along sides of pan.
6. Reduce heat to 350 degrees.
7. Mix cream cheese with dry ingredients. Add vanilla, egg yolks, and cream. Blend.
8. Beat the 5 egg whites until stiff peaks form. Fold into mixture. Pour into pie crust.
9. Bake for 45 minutes. Cool. Leave cake in oven for additional hour to cool.

Yield: One 9-inch cake

Happy Holidays!

Hag Semeach!

INDEX